"What's this?"
says Nicholas

Nicholas cannot go to school today. He has chickenpox. He sits at the desk with a computer. "I love technology," he says.

Nicholas sends an email to his dad. Dad is an architect in town.

Tap, tap, tap.

"I'm not at school today. I have chickenpox," he tells Dad.

Mum has to go to work
too. She's a mechanic.
She is good at fixing cars.

Mum makes a cup of chamomile tea and calls Grannie Chris.

"Yes, I can," says Grannie Chris. "He will need something for the spots. I will stop at the chemist on the way."

When Grannie Chris comes,
she and Nicholas play
"What's this?" on the laptop.

"What's this?" says Nicholas.
Grannie Chris thinks it is a
Christmas tree.

She's right! It is a Christmas tree.

"What's this?" says Nicholas.

Grannie Chris thinks it is an anchor.

She's right! It is an anchor.
"What's this?" says Nicholas.
Grannie Chris thinks it is an
orchestra.

She's right! It is an orchestra.
"What's this?" says Nicholas.
Grannie Chris thinks it's a
monarch butterfly.

She's right! It is a monarch
butterfly.

"What's this?" says Nicholas.

Grannie thinks it is a snake.

"I win!" says Nicholas.
"It's a chameleon."

Nicholas is starting to feel better. But all that technology has worn Grannie Chris out. Poor Grannie!

"What's this?" says Nicholas   Level 7, Set 2a, Text 95

Words to blend

Nicholas	school	technology
architect	mechanic	chamomile
Chris	chemist	Christmas
anchor	orchestra	monarch
chameleon	computer	email
butterfly	Grannie	chickenpox

17

"What's this?" says Nicholas

Before reading

Synopsis: Nicholas and Grannie Chris play a guessing game on the computer.

Review phonemes and graphemes: /ear/ ere, eer; /air/ are, ear, ere; /j/ ge, dge, g; /s/ c, ce, sc, se, st

Focus phoneme: /c/ **Focus grapheme:** ch

Book discussion: Look at the cover, and read the title together. Ask: *What kind of book do you think this is – fiction or non-fiction? Why do you think this? What do you think might happen in this book?*

Link to prior learning: Remind children that the sound /c/ as in 'cat' can also be spelled 'ch'. Turn to page 4 and ask children to find as many words as they can with this spelling of the /c/ sound (Nicholas, school, architect).

Vocabulary check: architect: a person who designs buildings.

Decoding practice: Display the words 'school', 'mechanic', 'Chris' and 'technology'. Can children circle the letter string that makes the /c/ sound, and read each word?

Tricky word practice: Display the word 'says'. Challenge children to circle the tricky part of this word ('ay' which makes the /e/ sound). Practise reading and writing this word.

After reading

Apply learning: Discuss the book. Ask: *What do you do when you can't go to school? Do you think 'What's this?' looks like a fun game?*

Comprehension

- Why can't Nicholas go to school? (He has chickenpox.)
- What does Nicholas' mum do for work? (She's a mechanic.)
- What was the last thing in the game of 'what's this?'? (a chameleon)

Fluency

- Pick a page that most of the group read quite easily. Ask them to reread it with pace and expression. Model how to do this if necessary.
- Challenge children to read Grannie Chris' words on page 8 as if she were really talking.
- Practise reading the words on page 17.

"What's this?" says Nicholas   Level 7, Set 2a, Text 95

Tricky words review

what	says	once
today	thought	love
have	something	comes
whole	again	do
many	ask	through